PREFACE

There are a lot of introductory books on frame relay, many of them longer and more detailed than this one. This little book, however, has been designed with one purpose in mind: to provide an easy-to-read introduction to frame relay for busy communications professionals who may know little about this rapidly emerging standard beyond the publicity it's getting in the communications industry.

Our aim is to give you enough information to enable you to ask the right questions of your network planners and vendors—not to overwhelm you with technobabble and unnecessary detail. You'll note, for example, there's no glossary: we've tried to write this frame relay introduction so you don't need one.

We assume, of course, that you have at least some knowledge of data communications and an even greater interest in keeping pace with the latest developments in the industry. (If you'd like a refresher on basics, refer to the first book in this series: *The Basics Book of Information Networking*.)

As you continue looking for ways to develop a successful strategy for enterprise networking in the 1990s, frame relay is one solution to consider. After a short introduction that provides a bit of background, our quick tour begins in Chapter 1 with a brief look at what frame relay is and why its emergence is important to many businesses worldwide. Chapter 2 discusses the benefits of frame relay. Chapter 3 shows where frame relay fits in with all those other communications standards you hear about. Chapter 4 tells you about the people behind frame relay—who's backing it, how, and why. Chapter 5 concludes with a look at some applications.

THE
BASICS
BOOK

of Frame Relay

Motorola Codex

**MOTOROLA
UNIVERSITY
PRESS**

ADDISON-WESLEY PUBLISHING COMPANY
Reading, Massachusetts • Menlo Park, California • New York
Don Mills, Ontario • Wokingham, England • Amsterdam
Bonn • Sydney • Singapore • Tokyo • Madrid • San Juan
Seoul • Milan • Mexico City • Taipei

The publisher offers discounts on this book when ordered in quantity for special sales.

For more information, please contact:
Corporate & Professional Publishing Group
Addison-Wesley Publishing Company
One Jacob Way
Reading, Massachusetts 01867

Text printed on recycled and acid-free paper

ISBN: 0-201-56377-0
10 11 12 13 14 15 16 17 18-CRW-99989796
Tenth printing, June 1996

THE
BASICS
BOOK

of Frame Relay

MOTOROLA UNIVERSITY PRESS

The Motorola Codex Basics Book Series
The Basics Book of Information Networking
The Basics Book of X.25 Packet Switching
The Basics Book of ISDN
The Basics Book of OSI and Network Management
The Basics Book of Frame Relay

TABLE OF CONTENTS

INTRODUCTION

It's no secret that the size, complexity, and configuration of the world's private communications networks are changing ever more rapidly. The reasons are by now familiar: growth in data traffic, a plethora of new applications such as Electronic Data Interchange (EDI), file transfers, facsimile, and Computer Aided Design/ Computer Aided Manufacturing (CAD/CAM), and the rise of personal computer networks—all resulting in the need to transmit large volumes of high-speed data in unpredictable patterns known as "bursts." This variability in traffic volume and frequency can make cost-effective transmission a real challenge.

There has, of course, been a significant improvement in the quality of telephone company lines and switched circuits, largely due to the widespread deployment of digital communications links. Concurrently, data processing equipment and data communications equipment have also become increasingly more sophisticated.

Tariffs are coming down, too, although in many cases bandwidth needs are accelerating faster than the cost of bandwidth is decreasing. So the search goes on for new ways of coping with these "bursty" applications at minimal cost, while improving end user response times and increasing throughput.

That's where frame relay comes in. Frame relay is an emerging network access protocol designed to accommodate bursty data applications. It is characterized by four important features:

1. High transmission speeds
2. Low network delay
3. High connectivity
4. Efficient bandwidth use

Frame relay is aimed at networks that use packet-oriented technologies for the transmission of data. It is specifically designed to address the problem of variable burst sizes and unpredictable traffic patterns.

We'll look at each of these points in detail as we go along.

Sounds great, you say. But why haven't I seen it in action? Don't worry. You will, and soon, because the first implementations of frame relay have already taken place. In the meantime, the two major standards bodies that are deciding how frame relay should be implemented have finalized technical work on frame relay standards. These organizations are the T1S1 Committee, accredited by the American National Standards Institute (ANSI), and the International Telegraph and Telephone Consultative Committee (CCITT). The CCITT is part of the United Nations and works with input from various national standards bodies (such as ANSI) to develop final, cohesive standards that vendors worldwide will agree to follow.

Is frame relay something you really need to know about? Perhaps, if your company needs to bring more data onto your wide area network (WAN). Today, most companies view an efficient network as a strategic corporate asset. The faster and more cost effectively information is sent, the greater the competitive advantage. Frame relay can play an important part in maximizing that advantage.

You might also be interested in frame relay if you want to cut the cost of running your company's WAN. Or if you want to reduce network life-cycle costs and keep the equipment you've already purchased around a little longer without adding line capacity. Or even if you need to improve the response time for some applications, or migrate easily to higher speeds for others.

Sounds good so far? Read on.

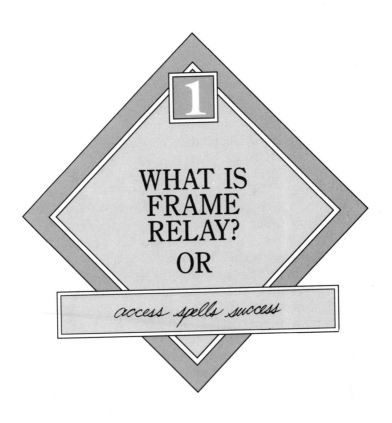

WHAT IS FRAME RELAY? OR

access spells success

Please bear with us a moment while we state the obvious, which will help clarify both the nature and the usefulness of frame relay. We have alluded to the tremendous growth in the use of personal computers. As a result, there has been a movement away from hierarchical terminal-to-host computing as people in companies discover how to exchange data with each other, as well as with computer and database facilities. In fact, host mainframes have now become database servers, accessible not only by dumb terminals but also by PCs and workstations.

Local area networks (LANs) interconnect these PCs on the desktop. But interconnecting LANs at different sites often requires the use of wide area services as well, and this is where new challenges emerge. First, users expect to interconnect LANs via wide area services yet still retain the same level of performance and responsiveness they enjoyed in their purely LAN environments. Second, WAN bandwidth is more expensive than LAN bandwidth. WAN circuits are typically thinner and longer, too—that is, they carry less traffic than LAN channels, with greater delay, thereby limiting throughput. So the real challenge is to optimize wide area services as a corporate network resource.

Complicating that challenge is another trend: the changing profile of data traffic. A variety of emerging applications, from large file transfers to graphics and imaging applications, are responsible for this change. To focus on imaging alone, doctors now use imaging to transfer X-rays and CAT scans, insurance agencies use it to transmit insurance claims, and banks use it to reduce paper. Each of these applications makes possible the accurate and timely exchange of critical information designed to benefit, respectively, the patient, the insurance subscriber, and the bank customer. These new applications as well as many older ones transmit high-speed (i.e., hundreds of thousands of bps), bandwidth-intensive bursts of information in unpredictable patterns and cannot tolerate excessive delays across the WAN links.

All these changes—the increase in bandwidth-intensive applications, unpredictable traffic patterns, and growing user demands—translate into a need for networks that can economically provide high-capacity bandwidth on demand. Frame relay is a network interface designed to help meet this need.

Now let's go back to our introductory definition and examine it more closely. In effect, we said **frame relay is an emerging network access protocol for bursty data applications.** If you take that definition apart, you begin to understand the advantages of frame relay.

To begin with, frame relay is a **protocol.** Just to recap, protocols, in data communications, at least, have nothing to do with diplomats, although they have a great deal to do with the behavior of data traffic within a network. A protocol is a set of agreed-on formats and procedures that govern the transfer of information between devices. They are the rules of the road that make communications work and ensure that the data received are identical to the data sent.

Today, most newer data communications protocols provide one or more layers of the Open Systems Interconnection (OSI) Reference Model, developed by the International Organization for Standardization (ISO). This defines a layered architecture in which overall data communications activities are partitioned into seven functional layers.

The key fact to note here is that the more layers of the OSI model that are supported, the more complex the protocols and, of curse, the more they do. (For a more detailed discussion of the OSI model, see our *Basics Book of Information Networking* or *Basics Book of X.25 Packet Switching.*)

As a protocol, frame relay provides capabilities both for the establishment of connections (calls) and for the transfer of data across those connections. Call setup occurs in the third, or network, layer of the OSI model, but once the connection is established, the main part of the job begins—the transfer of data. It is in this phase that protocols

The OSI Reference Model subdivides overall data communications activities into seven functional layers.

figure 1

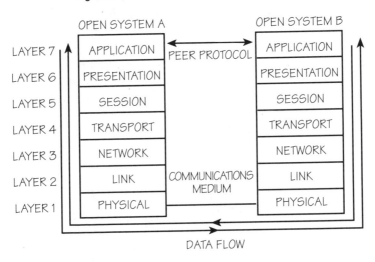

DATA FLOW

assert their differences. From this point on in frame relay, only part of layer two (the data link layer) and all of layer one (the physical layer) are used, and data transfer proceeds much more expeditiously than with more complex protocols.

Comparing frame relay with X.25—a protocol with which you may already be familiar—will help us keep this explanation basic. Both are data-only protocols: they do not work for voice or real-time video. In fact, frame relay evolved out of X.25, but there is a significant difference between the two.

Although X.25 uses the bottom three OSI layers during data transmission—the physical, data link, and network layers—frame relay (as we've seen) uses just the lower two, or more precisely, the lower one-and-one-half: the physical layer and part of the data link layer. This means X.25 performs error correction and retransmission functions, but frame relay performs error detection only (so it can drop bad frames), but not error correction. It leaves this task to the higher-level protocols used by the intelligent devices at each end of the network, which provide end-to-end data integrity. A typical example is IBM's System Network Architecture (SNA.)

Because frame relay relies on end-to-end protocols to perform retransmission and error recovery, there is less processing required at the network nodes and, consequently, less overall delay across the network. All

X.25 uses the bottom three OSI layers, but frame relay uses the lower one-and-one-half.

good frames are processed very quickly as they pass across the network interface. Frames in error are simply dropped; these are then retransmitted by the end systems. This capability enables

figure 2

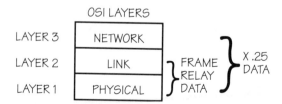

frame relay nodes to pass data traffic more rapidly, allowing higher traffic volumes and greater channel speeds to be provided without necessarily increasing equipment cost or size.

Frame relay, then, is concerned solely with what happens at the network interface: it is an **access** protocol that specifies a set of procedures governing the movement of data on and off the WAN. (In Chapter 4, we detail the specifications comprising the frame relay protocol and explore in depth concepts such as "committed burst size" and "rate enforcement.")

Like X.25, frame relay is a **packet-oriented** network access protocol, which leads into the second part of our definition—suitability for bursty data applications. Packet-oriented technologies play an important role in today's networks. Let's review briefly how these technologies work.

A time division multiplexer (TDM) divides bandwidth into fixed time slots and allocates one time slot to each of the channels feeding into the multiplexer. Thus, if a channel needs 64 Kbps of bandwidth, this amount of bandwidth is allocated and remains fixed even when there is no activity on the channel. No other channel can use the unused bandwidth. This means a large portion of bandwidth can often sit idle. It also means that if data traffic requirements are variable, there is no way to allocate more bandwidth to individual channels and improve response time.

Packet-oriented protocols, on the other hand, provide a way to allocate bandwidth intelligently to individual traffic streams on an as-needed basis instead of through fixed channel allocations. Instead of permanently setting aside bandwidth, such protocols group data into discrete packets or frames together with housekeeping information. This allows traffic from several sources to be logically multiplexed through a single interface into the network. Packets can be sent across the interface as soon as there is bandwidth available. When there is no traffic on a particular channel, no packets are sent and the bandwidth is free for use by other channels.

Packet switching, then, results in **statistical gain**: circuit switching can waste bandwidth, but packet switching conserves bandwidth by interleaving data from multiple sources and packing it onto the circuit wherever there is room. The difference can be illustrated by contrasting a circuit-switched T1/E1 network with a fast-packet T1/E1 network, as shown in Figure 3. The fast-packet network is ideally suited to traffic that varies widely in volume and frequency.

Chapter 3 shows that frame relay can work with either of these networks but that it's best suited to packet-based products. That's because frame relay expedites the movement of irregular bursts of data out into the wide area network.

Before we can appreciate how frame relay accomplishes this task, it will be helpful to put the concept of **bursty** traffic in a more familiar context. Remember the last time you were in a heavy traffic jam? You might have covered 10 miles in an hour. But if you watched your speedometer, you'd have found that you were mostly driving at zero miles per hour, with "bursts" of traveling at 30 miles per hour. Maybe the actual speed limit was 60 mph, adding to your frustration.

Frame relay is much easier on the nerves. It accommodates varying burst sizes (up to a point) and guarantees

In a circuit-switched T1/E1 network, bandwidth is divided into fixed channel allotments. In a packet-based T1/E1 network, on the other hand, bandwidth is allocated on an as-needed basis, making it more suitable for bursty applications.

figure 3

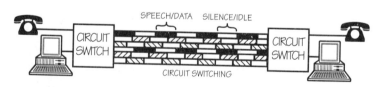

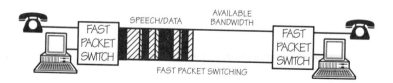

that if the "speed limit" is 60 mph, you'll get to travel a total of 60 miles in an hour. (But watch out if you try to go 61 miles in an hour!) All those caveats in parentheses may seem like cause for concern. But they are really nothing to worry about. As you'll see in Chapter 4, a well-designed frame relay network takes a few built-in limits fully into account.

For now, however, let's assume you have a well-designed frame relay network. What benefits can you hope to enjoy? Too many to enumerate here. They really deserve a chapter of their own.

Frame Relay in Brief

Frame relay refers to the technique of passing "frames" or blocks of information across a digital network interface using a connection number applied to each frame to distinguish individual connections. At the edges of the network, this number identifies the traffic source and ultimate destination. Routing is controlled on an end-to-end basis by the network, but link-to-link error correction and retransmissions are not performed. Instead, data integrity is guaranteed by higher-level protocols at each end of the network. (For example, X.25-LAPB can be used for this purpose.) In effect, frame relay allows data traffic to move rapidly along the network "highway," passing through switching nodes with a minimum amount of processing. As a result, it offers reduced throughput delays and supports data transmission at up to 2 Mbps today.

2

THE BENEFITS OF FRAME RELAY OR

less is more

By now you know broadly what frame relay is and in general what it does. Now it's time to chalk up some of the benefits frame relay can bring to your network *and* to your business.

In the preceding chapter we pointed out that networks have become strategic business tools and part of the infrastructure of many companies, particularly those trying to cut costs or expand into other countries, or both. Savvy users are demanding instant access to other users, applications, and/or computer resources. Those of you managing networks with data traffic are trying to fill everyone's needs by coming up with integrated and flexible multiapplication and multitechnology solutions. There are some good reasons to consider products with frame relay interfaces as part of your overall strategy.

Note first, however, that companies without extensive private networks or companies that want to supplement their private network with public services can also take advantage of frame relay via public service offerings. These are becoming increasingly available. Some interexchange carriers including WilTel, AT&T, MCI, and Sprint and value-added networks (VANs) such as CompuServe and, internationally, BT Tymnet, are already implementing frame relay interfaces to provide a public or hybrid solution. They are implementing the interface on T1, X.25, and central office switches. Some are positioning frame relay as part of their global networking services because it's based on an adopted international standard.

In Europe, the market for frame relay is still maturing: Telecom Finland was the first PTT to offer a national frame relay service, in 1991. BT and France TeleCom have announced frame relay services. Back in the United States, most of the Regional Bell Operating Companies (RBOCs) have been slow in pursuing frame relay, preferring instead **cell relay**. This differs from frame relay in that it prescribes a fixed amount of space for the transfer of information rather than permitting a variable amount of space depending on the volume of information to be transmitted. (The difference can be likened to the difference between circuit-switched time division multiplexing and bandwidth on demand, as shown in Figure 3 in the previous chapter.) Still, many RBOCs, such as NYNEX, are offering frame relay as well. Service providers will more than likely offer a variety of pricing plans, including fixed-rate, per-packet, and distance- and time-sensitive pricing.

This increased choice and flexibility is in itself one principal advantage offered by frame relay. Whether you choose to implement a public, private, or hybrid frame relay solution will of course depend on your particular network and business requirements. So it's important to work with someone who can help you evaluate those requirements knowledgeably. In general, however, frame relay offers a number of other key advantages that make it worth considering for the kind of bursty applications described in the last chapter.

IMPROVED NETWORK PERFORMANCE

This is the underlying network benefit that makes possible all the business benefits that follow. As we've seen, by minimizing processing delays, frame relay results in better response times and can support greater throughput. That's because it's a packet-oriented protocol. Bandwidth can be given to one user when others are idle; thus, bursts go through faster and you get more performance out of the same pipe than you would if you allocated fixed time slots.

IMPROVED PRODUCTIVITY/INCREASED CUSTOMER SATISFACTION

Because frame relay supports all kinds of data traffic and allows large volumes of bursty data to move through your network at faster speeds, the network can support greater throughput without increasing circuit capacity. This means network users, such as engineers exchanging CAD/CAM drawings from one LAN to another over the wide area network, or a customer making a bank transaction at a branch bank automatic teller machine, can accomplish their tasks more quickly. Faster response times, then, not only improve productivity, but can actually result in happier—and more loyal—customers.

DECREASED OPERATING COSTS/INCREASED RELIABILITY

Faster response times also decrease the cost per bit transmitted: frame relay's efficient design builds bandwidth savings into your network. At the same time, frame relay's single-line interface results in both bandwidth and hardware savings. Here's how. In many of today's high-speed backbone networks without frame relay, a separate physical port and circuit can be required for every possible connection across the network. Like X.25, however, frame relay supports multiple virtual connections on a single-line interface at the network access point, eliminating the need for multiple access lines and minimizing the number of port interfaces required.

Eliminating the multiple physical connections between end points and significantly simplifying the network topologies currently deployed in many large networks can translate to literally thousands of dollars in savings every month. Or, to put it more succinctly, shared pipes mean lower costs. Moreover, by reducing hardware requirements (and separate connections), the network also becomes more reliable.

Frame relay reduces operating costs by eliminating the need for multiple access lines and minimizing the number of port interfaces required.

figure 4

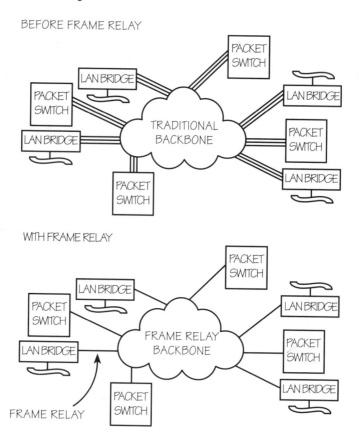

EASE OF MIGRATION/RESOURCE OPTIMIZATION

Frame relay enables you to protect the investment you've already made in existing network equipment because it complements products already in place. To give just one example, frame relay can provide a cost-effective, high-performance interface for X.25-based or SNA-based traffic into your backbone network. In many cases, you will be able to add it to many X.25 PADs and switches and to LAN bridge and router equipment with just a simple software upgrade. (In Chapter 3 we examine some of these complementary relationships in greater detail.)

Also, because frame relay is based on standards, you can be sure it will give you a clear migration path for network expansion. You won't be locked into using equipment from one vendor, but will have choices. Today, for example, there are already more than 60 suppliers developing frame relay–based products.

LIFE-CYCLE COST SAVINGS/MAXIMUM RETURN ON NETWORK INVESTMENT

All the above benefits lead inevitably to this principal business benefit. By using frame relay in appropriate applications, you not only can save money now, but also in the future. Once you begin to compute the cost in overall hardware (figuring in the human resources needed to manage that hardware) and lines currently required to connect your remote devices, and then estimate the additional hardware and line costs you expect to incur over the next 5 years, and then . . . well, you can begin to appreciate the importance of assessing the implementation of frame relay in your network.

Just how *does* frame relay work with existing network technologies? Let's see.

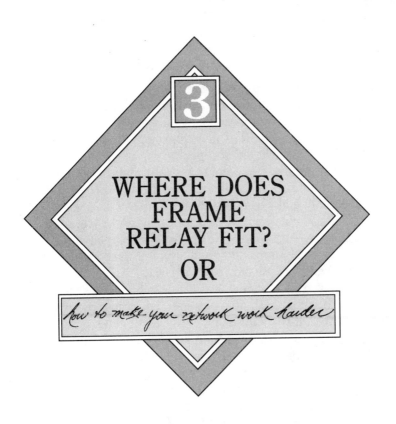

3

WHERE DOES FRAME RELAY FIT? OR

How to make your network work harder

Getting acquainted with what frame relay is and how it works is only the first step toward learning where this data access protocol fits into your network. The next step is to see how frame relay meshes with other protocols, interfaces, and networking technologies. In a wide area network (WAN) environment, frame relay can provide access to a backbone network by interconnecting a broad range of feeder products, such as LAN bridges and routers, or X.25 PADs and switches. In many cases, frame relay can improve on the many good qualities of these other protocols or technologies and help you further optimize your network resources.

FRAME RELAY AND CELL RELAY

Emerging wideband and broadband networks are evolving away from time-division switching and transmission toward an approach variously called fast-packet switching, cell relay, and ATM (asynchronous transfer mode). These are all packet-based protocols, which means (if you need a quick reminder) that information is transferred in packets of small (usually fixed) sizes. Actually, frame relay and cell relay are subsets of fast-packet technology, but they are not mutually exclusive, as we'll see shortly. And what's ATM? A cell-relay standard that supports voice, data, image, and video. It is at the core of emerging broadband ISDN services, which we'll touch on later in this chapter.

Because both are packet-oriented protocols, frame relay and cell relay make powerful teammates. Both intelligently allocate bandwidth on an as-needed basis. What's the difference? Frame relay is a network access protocol for data traffic only, whereas cell relay is a switching method designed to carry data, voice, and video traffic across a high-speed wide area backbone network.

The advantages of frame relay become really significant in a cell-relay network. Together they offer the best of two worlds: a standard interface to existing equipment and efficient movement across the WAN. More specifically, the dynamic bandwidth allocation that starts at the frame relay interface is carried on through the cell-relay network. Frame relay data is also able to take advantage of the logical connectivity and routing characteristics of the cell-relay backbone network. Like frame relay, cell relay is cost effective because it minimizes processing in the intermediate nodes.

Figure 5 shows how frame relay can be implemented to bring data traffic onto a cell-relay backbone. In fact, in one typical example (a mapping application) the advantage of a frame relay interface in reducing delays is quite dramatic compared with other access technologies. In the application as originally designed, data went out at 56 Kbps over an X.25 backbone. Each transmission took almost 4 minutes. After implementing a T1 backbone with multiple 56 Kbps circuits, transmission time was reduced by more than half. But adding a

768 Kbps frame relay interface to the same T1 backbone further decreased the transmission time nearly tenfold without affecting network availability. The chart below summarizes the results of this evolutionary process: **The bursty nature of frame relay traffic is ideally suited to a cell-relay network.**

figure 5

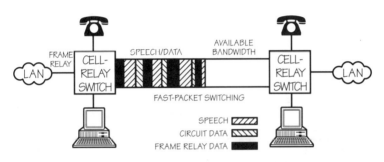

Backbone	Access	Transmission Time
X.25	56 Kbps X.25	3 min. 50 sec.
T1	Multiple 56 Kbps	1 min. 45 sec.
T1	768 Kbps frame relay	0 min. 11 sec.

It is important to note, however, that implementation of a frame relay solution could occur only because end systems provided necessary error recovery.

FRAME RELAY AND X.25

Don't let the preceding example mislead you. Frame relay and X.25 also can work very well together, each fulfilling a critical role at different points in the network.

This should come as no surprise, of course, because both are packet-oriented network access protocols that are virtual circuit based. (Virtual circuits, in case you've forgotten, are logical rather than physical connections between a pair of end points. Through virtual circuits, multiple logical connections can be established across any physical path.)

A little history may help you appreciate the network evolution that now enables X.25 users to add the advantages of frame relay to those provided by X.25.

When X.25 was originally designed, its error recovery and flow control capabilities were essential to keeping data running smoothly over a WAN. Error recovery was necessary because analog networks were noisy and digital networks had not yet attained today's high level of quality. Flow control was also critical: networks ran data at 64 Kbps or less, microprocessors were slower, and computer memory was expensive.

Now, with today's high-quality, high-speed digital transmission facilities, more processing can be accomplished in the hardware itself, and today's sophisticated computer technology provides for more performance. This means that X.25's error recovery and flow control aren't always needed within the network, although its use outside the frame relay network significantly complements the capabilities of frame relay because many of the original circumstances still apply there.

In fact, the combination may be ideal. Frame relay provides fast, efficient access to a backbone network. And today's X.25 products can provide end-to-end error recovery for asynchronous protocols, protocol conversion for a wide variety of nonstandard proprietary protocols (not provided by today's frame relay products), and a large selection of management services, such as collection of billing statistics.

Today's installed base of X.25 devices is huge, and now these networks can start to benefit from frame relay, too. Take, for example, an organization that uses X.25 devices at remote locations and concentrates them onto a private backbone network through a frame relay interface. The X.25 devices act as cost-effective, high-performance entry points that correct errors on low-speed analog tail circuits. Then frame relay provides high-speed access for all data from the X.25 feeders into the backbone.

Thus, by reducing dependence on switches and subnetworks, frame relay can ease the migration of an existing data network and provide a higher throughput of data onto an integrated voice/data network. Translated into simple business terms, this means you don't have to change all the equipment in your network to get better network performance. If you like to save money—and who doesn't?—here's a great way to do it. (We take a closer look at the implementation of an X.25/frame relay network in Chapter 5.)

FRAME RELAY AND CIRCUIT SWITCHING

Until now, we've ignored another type of switching that's still a significant part of the network scene—circuit switching. Many of you have circuit switches in your networks, so you'll be glad to know that frame relay can serve as a data access protocol in a circuit-switched environment. It is particularly useful where high-speed circuits are used to access public networks using public network time division multiplexing (TDM) standards (such as T1/D4 or E1/G.704).

A circuit switch allows a fixed amount of bandwidth for each voice and data channel connected to the network. This means that the frame relay interface can effectively handle traffic bursts up to the amount of bandwidth allocated for its use. Because data traffic from several sources can be aggregated, statistically frame relay provides more efficient use of the allocated channel than the circuit switch alone can do.

Figure 6 will help you to see what we mean. In handling a frame relay application, a digital circuit might be configured like this: half the bandwidth is allocated to individual voice and circuit data channels and half is given over to a single pool of bandwidth for frame relay virtual circuits. This provides several benefits.

Although a circuit switched network can accommodate frame relay traffic, delays can result when bursts of data exceed the designated bandwidth.

figure 6

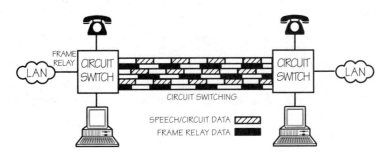

19

First, there is more bandwidth available for frame relay bursts than is provided by separate data channels. Second, data traffic in the frame relay circuit can be switched independently of the purely circuit traffic, allowing the possibility of data rerouting on circuit failure. However, when bursts of frame relay traffic require more bandwidth than is designated—as is often the case—not all the digital circuit bandwidth can be accessed. Thus, depending on actual circuit configuration, data may have to spend more time "waiting in line," so there can be more delays with this approach.

Moreover, the fact that two different switching techniques are in use may introduce additional delays at intermediate nodes: traffic arriving at nodes must be demultiplexed using circuit switching technology, switched via the frame relay component, then remultiplexed out again. This improves circuit use but may result in additional delays.

FRAME RELAY AND LAN INTERCONNECTIVITY

There are many benefits of using frame relay to link LANs across a WAN. In fact, Motorola Codex and other suppliers of LAN interconnection equipment view the development of the frame relay interface standard as key to cutting LAN interconnecion costs while reducing the severity of LAN routing problems.

To see why this is important, let's look back in time. (If you've read Chapter 1, you can skip this and the following paragraph.) In the early 1980s, when packet switching began to take hold, the number of LANs in companies worldwide was minuscule. Because there weren't many LANs, there was little need for a technology that would transmit the large volumes of bursty data between LANs over WANs.

Soon, however, people started to equate decentralized processing with increased productivity. The number of LANs in departments of companies worldwide exploded, and now there are a lot of LANs and an enormous need to interconnect them efficiently.

This is where frame relay comes in. Frame relay provides a high-performance, single-line interface onto the WAN for LAN bridges and routers. The resulting benefits are impressive.

- LANs gain high performance access into the WAN.
- The backbone links benefit from statistical gain. Because idle characters are suppressed, only actual user information is transmitted, and bandwidth is dynamically shared among users.
- The single-line interface cuts hardware and line costs.
- Frame relay indirectly enables LANs to take advantage of the resiliency designed into today's private WANs. This can be advantageous because LAN routers, typically designed with LAN protocols in mind, frequently do not support WAN realities.
- Many different LAN bridges and routers can use common backbone network facilities when they implement frame relay.
- LANs can now be controlled and managed from the WAN's perspective.

In a typical LAN interconnect application, shown in the first diagram in Figure 4, LAN bridges and routers operate by connecting a number of fixed leased-line circuits between interconnected LAN devices. Although this provides connectivity between the LANs, it adds substantial line and hardware costs or may force the use of lower speed circuits to reduce these costs.

In the second diagram in Figure 4, the frame relay interface on the network provides higher-speed interconnection for LANs. The backbone in this case can be a private digital network or a public frame mode data service. The single-line access reduces line charges and hardware costs.

As bandwidth requirements grow, networks that cannot economically transfer large bursts of data will not meet users' future requirements and their technologies will rapidly become obsolete. Frame relay allows you to give your LANs access to each other through a high-speed backbone. Faster networks, happier users. Right?

FRAME RELAY AND ISDN

As most of you know by now, Integrated Services Digital Network (ISDN) is an all-digital network that allows users to access a range of today's separate communications services by means of a single set of interface standards. Its goal is to provide universal end-to-end digital connectivity, enabling users to move data, voice, image, facsimile, and more, either separately or simultaneously over the network.

ISDN interfaces are designed to support both bearer capabilities (i.e., carry data, voice, or video traffic) and signaling information. Today, only narrowband services, using a combination of circuit-switched and low-speed packet technology, have been implemented. These provide speeds up to 2 Mbps. In the future, fast-packet-based, high-speed broadband ISDN services will be available.

Frame relay, which is roughly based on ISDN's data link layer protocol for signaling called Link Access Protocol D (LAPD) was originally intended to be an ISDN bearer service. When and if ISDN makes sense for your business, frame relay can be used to carry data across ISDN services offering circuit-switched connections at 64 Kbps, 384 Kbps, and 1536 Kbps. In other words, frame relay is compatible and complementary with ISDN.

(To learn more about ISDN, refer to *The Basics Book of ISDN.*)

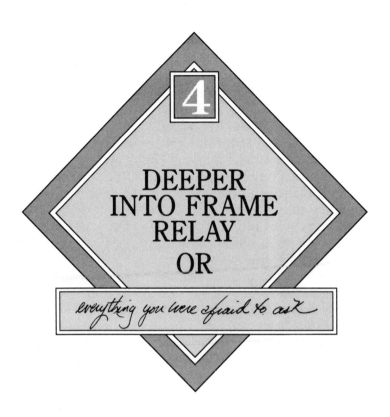

4

DEEPER INTO FRAME RELAY

OR

everything you were afraid to ask

In this chapter we explore the frame relay protocol to see what makes it work.

Developing standards has become standard practice in the data communications world. As we mentioned in Chapter 1, a standard is a set of agreements among industry participants that represent the functions and features of a technology and how these work together. Why is this desirable? So you can pick and choose your equipment vendor on your own criteria, knowing that the equipment you select will work with other equipment and services based on the same standard. For example, if Company A and Company B both follow the blueprint for a technology's standard when placing that technology into their products, then the equipment they build independently should work well together.

Right now, two important committees are carving out frame relay standards. In the United States, the work is handled by the ANSI-accredited technical committee known as T1S1. (Motorola Codex, by the way, chaired ANSI's T1S1.1 Working Group on services and architecture during the development of the frame relay description and contributed many of the ideas that led to the frame relay standards.) T1S1, in turn, gives input on frame relay to CCITT Study Groups XI and XVIII. The Introduction of this book gives background on who ANSI and the CCITT are.

Technical work on the frame relay standards was finalized in 1991. As with any new communications standards, however, equipment suppliers are still in a period of transition. Yet if you ask, What if I buy equipment now, during this time of transition? don't worry. For the most part, the suppliers who implemented prestandard interfaces waited until the standards were already far enough along to ensure broad compatibility among products. For software-oriented devices, further changes will be made in equipment already in the field through simple upgrades, provided your supplier is committed to supporting the final standards.

THE FRAME RELAY STANDARDS

The CCITT has decided to break down the functions and features of frame relay into five separate standards—service description, congestion management, core aspects, access signaling, and data link control.

The **service description** standard (ANSI T1.606, CCITT I.233) outlines the overall purpose and general features of frame relay. These were covered in Chapters 1 and 2.

The **congestion management** standard (ANSI T1.606, Addendum 1; CCITT I.370) defines speed and burstiness and describes how the network and end-user devices handle an overabundance of data traffic.

Traffic? Congestion? Rush hour? It's similar. The movement of data through a network sometimes needs traffic signs to indicate when it should stop and go. But for the time being we'll skip the heart of the matter—frame relay's **core aspects** (ANSI T1.618, CCITT Q.922)—to describe the fourth and fifth standards within the frame relay specifications. **Access signaling** (ANSI T1.617, CCITT Q.933) specifies a protocol for establishing and releasing switched frame relay virtual calls and provides a means to inform users of permanent virtual circuits of failure and restoral. The **data link control** standard (ANSI: no standard planned, CCITT Q.922) provides an *optional* end-to-end mechanism for ensuring the correct delivery of information across the network. This is designed for implementation in end-user devices and is not implemented in a frame relay network for the purpose of carrying user traffic because end-user devices usually rely on other protocols to ensure data accuracy.

Now to the heart of frame relay, its core aspects.

The chart in Figure 7 shows the format in which frame relay (FR) is laid out. This format roughly conforms to the **high-level data link control (HDLC)** frame format, which is common to SNA, X.25, and ISDN (remember LAPD?) among others.

As you can see from Figure 7, the FR format has six different components. Each is responsible for a specific function.

On each end of the FR format, you will find flags that delimit where the data frame starts and ends. The central

The format for frame relay data roughly conforms to the HDLC frame format.

figure 7

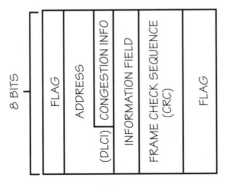

part of the FR format is the **Data Link Connection Identifier,** also known as **DLCI.** The DLCI distinguishes separate virtual circuits across each access connection. This allows data coming into a frame relay network node to be sent across the interface by specifying a DLCI rather than a destination address. At the network node, this connection specification is confirmed. If the specification is in error, the frame is discarded. If not, the frame is relayed to its destination.

Now we arrive at the congestion information field of the format. This is where bits relating to congestion control are stored. If the network is experiencing congestion, it is because several data sources are contending for the same bandwidth and are generating bursty and unpredictable data traffic. But hold on! (you're thinking), you've been saying all along that frame relay is designed specifically for this kind of traffic.

So we have, and so it is. To see how frame relay handles the situation, it will help first to look at why it happens. One reason is that frame relay allows users to send more data than the network reserves for them. This takes advantage of gaps in traffic and therefore permits the network to make gains from the statistical nature of that traffic. However, designing for statistical gain can lead to occasional overload. Each source is allocated a committed information rate and committed burst size, which allows all data sources to begin transmitting at the same time without congestion. However, each source can try to exceed its committed rate to take advantage of unused bandwidth. When too many sources contend for this available but limited bandwidth, congestion occurs.

OK, we admit we sneaked in some new terms in that last paragraph—which brings us to the discussion of committed burst size and rate enforcement that we promised you in Chapter 1. Why is this important to you? Because to be an informed consumer of frame relay, you need to understand the concept of rate for the same reason that you need to understand the concepts of weight and volume when you go to the supermarket to buy butter and milk. (Imagine being asked to buy milk without knowing the difference between a quart or litre and a gallon.)

Here's how it works. Let's return to our opening analogy of a traffic jam. Only now let's conceive of a highway system that permits you to travel 60 miles during any 1-hour period. In fact, the rules of the road stipulate that you're *guaranteed* a distance of 60 miles in any 1-hour period—but no more than that. Should you try to exceed that committed rate, you'll be ticketed. However, let's say you have a car that will only stand still or go 90 miles per hour. To travel your 60 miles in 60 minutes, you must sit still for a total of 20 minutes and drive at 90 mph for a total of 40 minutes. If you're ticketed, rather than having to go to court and pay a fine, you can continue toward your destination, but if there's a traffic jam, your car is forced off the highway into a ditch. Frame relay traffic works the same way. The guaranteed rate of 60 miles per hour corresponds to what is called a **committed information rate (CIR);** that is, the rate (expressed in bits per second) at which the network agrees to transfer data. The speed at which the car actually travels (90 mph) corresponds to the access rate—the rate of the physical connection between the user equipment and the network. The 60 miles corresponds to the **committed burst size** (B_c)— the maximum number of bits that the network agrees to transfer during any measurement interval (T), which in our example happens to be 1 hour. Thus the "magic formula" in frame relay is:

$$T = B_c/CIR.$$

In our invented example, T = 60 miles/60 miles per hour = 1 hour. In other words, you will require 1.5 hours to go 90 miles, even though your car is capable of going 90 miles in one hour. Thus, for a network with a committed burst size of 32 kilobytes (256 kilobits) and a committed information rate of 64 Kbps:

$$T = (256 \text{ kilobits})/(64 \text{ Kbps}) = 4 \text{ seconds.}$$

Thus, the network will make its best effort to deliver 32 Kbytes over any 4-second period, or, to put it another way, will support an average user rate of 64 kbps averaged over a 4-second period.

Frame relay networks can use this notion of rate to implement **rate enforcement** at the user interface. Rate enforcement means that frames in excess of CIR will be carried only if bandwidth is available and discarded if insufficient bandwidth is available. A **discard eligibility (DE) bit** can be *set* in low-priority frames so that they are discarded first in the event of frame loss. This DE bit is *set* by the frame relay network in any frames received in excess of CIR, because the network assumes anything that exceeds the CIR is low priority. The DE bit can also be set by the end-user equipment if it knows that some frames are more important than others.

How does the terminal equipment know when the network is congested? By any one of several methods. From the congestion information field, a **forward explicit congestion bit (FECN)**—which is often used with protocols like DECnet—sends a signal to the receiving or destination end point, advising it to slow down the receipt of information. (The destination device measures the density of the FECN bits and, if the density threshold is exceeded, it reduces the "credits" granted to the sending device, which is then forced to reduce its rate.)

Alternatively, a **backward explicit congestion bit (BECN)**—usually used with SNA-type traffic—goes to the transmitting or source end point and advises it to slow down the sending of information immediately.

A couple of other important points should be made before leaving the topic of congestion. First, the implementation of FECN and BECN is called *explicit* congestion management. Some end-to-end protocols use FECN, while others use BECN. Both work well, but they are usually mutually exclusive options in end-user equipment.

Second, FECN and BECN are advisory only. They help terminal equipment match what is being sent to what the network can carry. But they can be ignored. For that reason, all frame relay networks also provide *implicit* congestion detection, which ultimately relies on the protocols in the end systems to detect and deal with the problem. Briefly, when congestion results in data frames being discarded, user equipment capable of detecting frame loss can infer that the loss was due to congestion and reduce its rate. Implicit congestion management is less effective than explicit because it always happens too late and requires a more drastic reaction by intelligent end devices. With explicit congestion management, a congestion condition is identified and corrected before it becomes critical. (TCP/IP is an example of a protocol suite that only implements implicit congestion control.)

Voila! Our traffic problem is solved. Rate enforcement ensures that a network never gets so congested that it can't meet its committed information rate, and explicit and implicit congestion notification make sure that users who choose to take their chances by transmitting in excess of CIR have the opportunity to slow down to match the available network bandwidth.

Next, the **Information Field** of the FR format in Figure 7 contains the actual information transmitted. The maximum allowed length of this information field can vary, depending on the design requirements of the network, from 262 to 8000 or more octets. (A reminder: an octet is an 8-bit byte.) *Beware: If your network does not support an information field of at least 1600 octets, you won't be able to carry many kinds of LAN traffic across the frame relay network.*

The next field—**Frame Check Sequence (FCS)**—is where the error checking takes place. Frame relay uses the error-checking technique known as **Cyclic Redundancy Check** or **CRC.** The frame relay CRC generates two bytes that go into the end of the frame to detect bad data. They do so by using an algebraic method to generate a unique bit pattern, which is recalculated at the far end. If the frame check sequence at the source matches the FCS at the destination, it means that the frame's integrity has (in most cases) been preserved.

When frame relay does discover a frame error, it merely drops the frame. As we've seen, it doesn't go through the process of requesting a resending of data if it finds errors in the transmission, but leaves this task up to the LAN station, X.25 switch, or other intelligent devices connected to the network.

That brings us back to the flag field in the FR format, which signals the end of our transmission and of this chapter.

**FRAME RELAY
APPLICATIONS
OR**

enough talk, now show me

Whether you're in manufacturing, financial services, government, or many other business sectors, you probably have applications that would benefit from frame relay. Frame relay is ideal for networks that handle:

- Information Systems (IS) applications
- Client server computing
- CAD/CAM applications
- LAN-to-LAN applications
- Graphics
- Facsimile
- Electronic data interchange (EDI)
- Imaging applications

- Electronic mail
- Other applications that generate bursty traffic

Brief descriptions follow of two hypothetical companies and how they use frame relay to take advantage of the benefits referred to in Chapter 2. Of course, this is only a small sample of applications for frame relay. But we hope they will pique your interest and help you think about how frame relay might fit into your own organization's network.

STREAMLINING GLOBAL CONNECTIONS: A PRIVATE NETWORK FRAME RELAY APPLICATION

Engineering design groups, one in Detroit and one in Lansing, Michigan, are working together on a project, using CAD/CAM to develop an engine. Engineers in the work groups communicate several times a day with each other over the network backbone. They frequently share information regarding the product's specifications and design with two manufacturing groups, one in a Detroit suburb and one in Munich, Germany. In addition, all the groups send weekly updates about the project's progress to headquarters in downtown Chicago.

Previously, a bottleneck was created when engineers and managers on LANs tried to move data onto the backbone at the same time. Transmission delay was long because there was no network access protocol capable of effectively handling the bursty, unpredictable data traffic generated from the LANs. Development slowed, and employees became frustrated.

Figures 8 and 9 show how frame relay solved the problem.

Figure 8 shows the configuration of the network without frame relay. Each work group has its own LAN. The LAN routers support CAD/CAM, imaging, PC and workstation applications, and feed into T1/E1 multiplexers. X.25 packet switches support terminal networks in the two manufacturing facilities and are connected to an X.25 packet switch at corporate headquarters, which supports three host computers.

In the past, multiple lines had to be deployed from the X.25 packet switches and the LAN routers to the cell-relay nodes to achieve end-to-end connectivity between all the end points and allow each location to communicate with all the others. No longer.

Before frame re-lay, this manufac-turer had to deploy multiple lines from the X.25 packet switches and the LAN routers to the cell-relay nodes.

figure 8

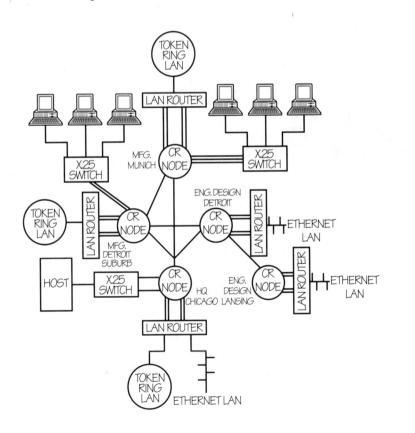

When frame relay was combined with cell relay on the network (Figure 9), the network could handle the bursty, unpredictable traffic from the LANs. Productivity between the work groups jumped as response time on the network dropped substantially.

Thus, by providing a single-line interface between end points and relying on end-user devices to handle most of the error processing, frame relay eliminated many lines, dramatically reduced hardware costs, simplified network design, and maximized bandwidth availability. The bottom line: it not only saved the company money but also improved network performance, thereby resulting in increased productivity and shorter times to get to market.

> After implementing frame relay, the network could handle the bursty, unpredictable traffic from the LANs while eliminating the multiple lines previously required.

figure 9

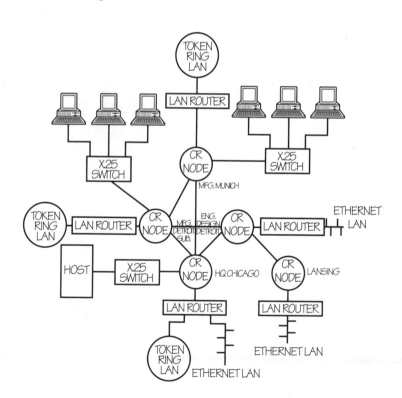

ECONOMIZING ON LAN CONNECTIONS: A PUBLIC NETWORK FRAME RELAY APPLICATION

A large manufacturer with offices around the United States was looking for a faster, more cost-effective way to link its LANs in various cities. It found one in frame relay.

Formerly the company used TDM-based carrier services to send its LAN data between offices in various cities. As shown in Figure 10, the company relied on a DACS network with Fractional T1 and T1 services between locations. Each link had to be sized to support the maximum burst size between those sites. For example, between routers A, B, and C the maximum burst size was 256 Kbps, requiring 256 Kbps (Fractional T1) service. Between routers D and E, Before implementing frame relay, the network had to be configured for maximum traffic requirements.

figure 10

DACS NETWORK

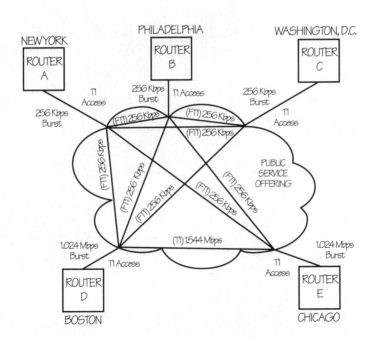

however, the burst size was 1.024 Mbps. But because the interexchange carrier does not support this service, the company had to rent a 1.544 Mbps link.

With frame relay, the manufacturer found that the same network could be provided but at a much lower cost. The reason is simple: although in the traditional TDM environment the network had to be configured for *maximum* traffic requirements, a frame relay environment allowed the company to configure for *minimum* traffic requirements and still retain the bandwidth needed for large bursts of data.

The network shown in Figure 11 is the same as the TDM network with the difference that service is provided through frame relay permanent virtual connections (PVCs). The manufacturer

After implementing frame relay, the network could be configured for minimum traffic requirements and still accommodate large bursts of data.

figure 11

FRAME RELAY NETWORK

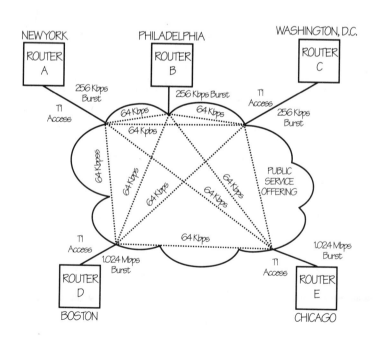

has four 64-Kbps PVC connections at each node, with A, B, and C capable of bursting to 256 Kbps and D and E capable of bursting to 1.024 Mbps.

In this particular example, using a frame relay interface saved the company 40 percent in transmission charges (based on tariffs and distances involved for the circuits between these cities). Of course, similar comparisons between private frame relay and TDM networks supporting multiple applications and traffic types yield similar results.

INDEX